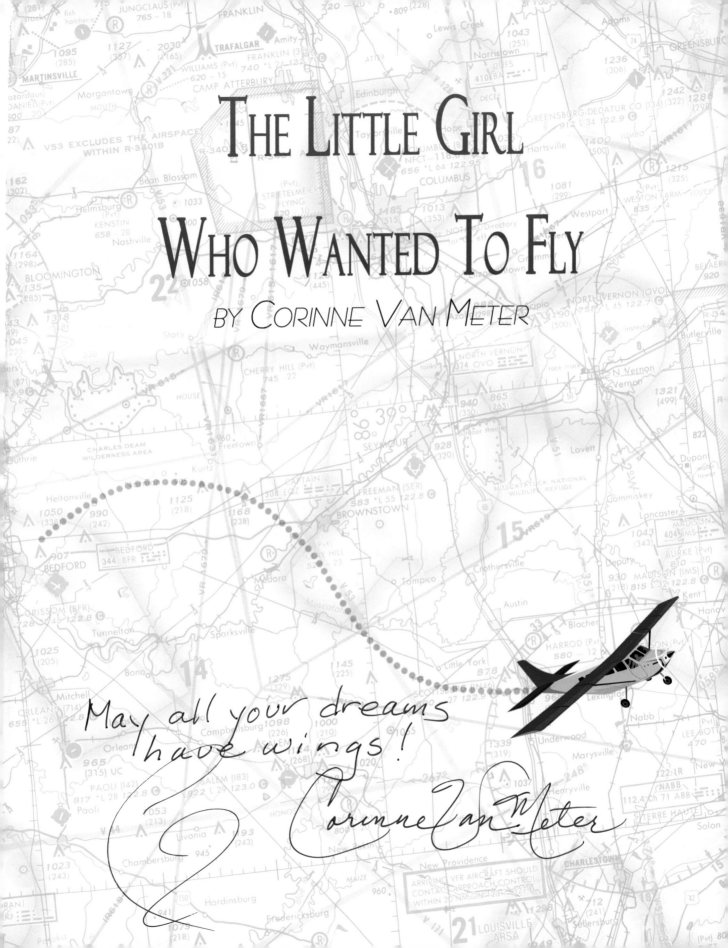

THE LITTLE GIRL
WHO WANTED TO FLY

BY CORINNE VAN METER

May all your dreams have wings !

Corinne Van Meter

Victoria Press
Copyright © 2013 Corinne Van Meter
Cover Design: Tor Lowry
ISBN: 0615774490
ISBN-13: 978-0615774497
Printed in the United States of America

This book is dedicated
to a child's dream . . .

*All possibilities rest within your dreams,
and it is you who holds the power
to awaken them.*
~ Corinne Van Meter

"It doesn't really matter
what age you are,
it matters what you think
and how you feel."

Vicki Van Meter
Time Magazine
October 1993

There was a little girl named Vicki who dreamed of being an astronaut. When she played, she pretended to be an airplane. When she sat in school, she looked out the window and imagined she was a bird. When she slept, Vicki danced among the stars.

When Vicki told her father about her dream, he listened to her. He took her to the town's small airport and signed her up for an airplane ride to see if she really liked to fly.

When they got home, Vicki told her mother that she was going to take a flying lesson soon. Her mother was shocked, but when Vicki shared her dream, she listened to the little girl's heart and said, "I believe you, Vicki. You can fly!"

On the day of Vicki's first lesson, the skies were clear and the sun was shining brightly. She went back to the airport and climbed into a little plane. The instructor showed her how to start the plane, how to take it off the ground, how to fly high, how to fly low, how to **bank the plane**, and then he said, "Go ahead, take the wheel, Vicki! You can fly!" Vicki knew inside that she *could* fly, so she took the wheel and she flew!"

Vicki decided she wanted to learn more, so she went to special classes with adults who wanted to learn how to fly, too. Some were farmers, some were big businessmen, some brought doughnuts, and some even smoked cigarettes!

She listened and she learned how to be safe when she flew. She went to lots of classes, she read her **private pilot ground school** book, she studied, she answered questions, and when Vicki took her final test . . .

Private Pilot

Ground School Test

FAIL   ☒

PASS   ☐

. . . she failed it!

"But," she said, "I *know* I can fly!" So, she took the classes all over again. She listened carefully. She read more. She studied harder. She even ate more doughnuts! She answered all the teacher's questions, and when Vicki took the final test again . . .

. . . she passed it with flying colors!

Her instructor said, "If you can fly, then fly!" So, that's just what she did. Vicki flew in an air show in her hometown. She flew to another city to visit her cousins, and she even flew to her big sister's high school graduation far away over the mountains.

Vicki was so happy when she flew! Her friends could hardly believe it, but they saw that it was true, and then she thought about a new goal . . . *I'd like to fly across the United States of America so that people will see that even little kids can fly if they want to, like me!*

So she prepared by studying big maps on her walls, she made lots of calculations, and practiced her flying until one day . . . she was ready!

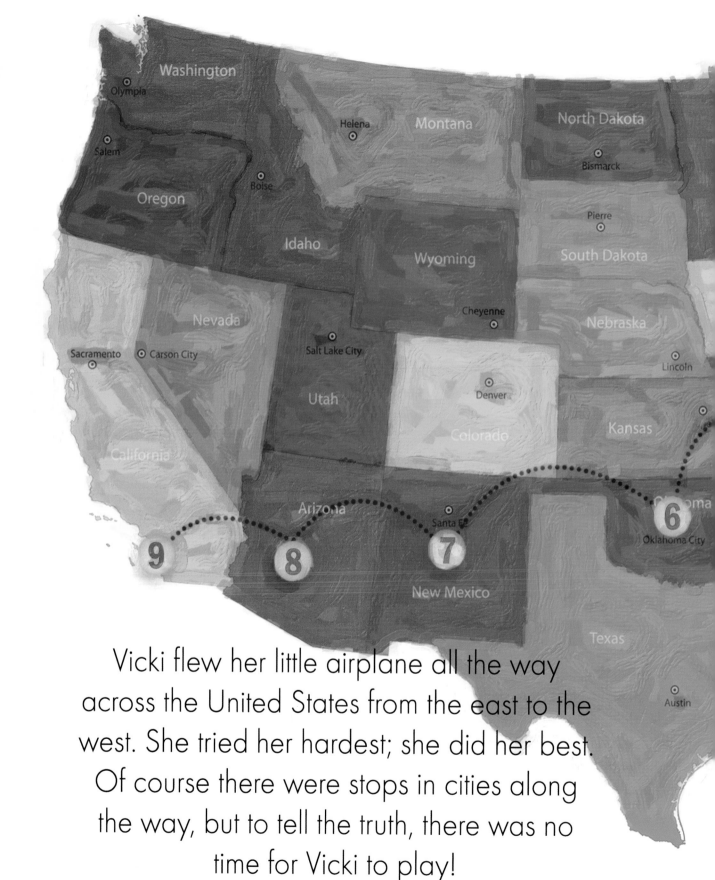

Vicki flew her little airplane all the way across the United States from the east to the west. She tried her hardest; she did her best. Of course there were stops in cities along the way, but to tell the truth, there was no time for Vicki to play!

FUEL STOPS

1. Meadville, PA
2. Augusta, ME
3. Harrisburg, PA
4. Columbus, OH
5. St. Louis, MO
6. Oklahoma City, OK
7. Albuquerque, NM
8. Phoenix, AZ
9. San Diego, CA

People heard about it on TV and in the news, and they could hardly believe it was true, but Vicki showed them all what little kids can do! Everywhere she stopped, the people came from far and near to see the little girl, to see her and cheer. Vicki talked so easily and told the crowds, "It was a challenge for me," and everyone was proud.

2,900 MILES LATER...

g pilot Victoria Van Meter with her Cessna 172 and plenty of media attention at Montgomery Field yesterd

HIGHFLIER AT 11

Youngest girl to fly cross-country sets sights on outer spac

ACK WILLIAMS
Writer

ntil yesterday, Meadville, Pa., was content to be known for such practical, down-to-earth products as Talon Zip-Channel Lock Pliers and a modest collec-f tool-and-dye shops.

w, the town of less than 14,000 has a

girl ever to pilot an airplane across the United States.

Vicki concluded the final leg of the 2,900-mile flight when her green-and-mustard-striped Cessna 172 settled smoothly onto the sun-baked tarmac yesterday at Montgomery Field shortly after 1:30 p.m.

An aspiring astronaut who earns mostly A's

She probably could have done w too, considering she hadn't had m than five hours of sleep a night sin Augusta, Maine, on Monday and h had been doing flipflops the day be

But amid national news crews, taries and their representatives be and cheering spectators, she exud

After her trip, she flew to the Johnson Space Center and showed everyone that she could land a space shuttle, it really could be done! The people and reporters asked, "What's next, what's next?" and Vicki thought about her next goal and said, "I think I'll fly across the Atlantic. First I'll fly to Iceland, then I'll land in Scotland. Next, I'll fly on to England, France, and Germany. Yes, that's the plan!"

That was the plan and that was the promise. Vicki promised herself that she'd show them all how it could be done, so she started preparing and everyone said, "Wow, she's really going to do it!"

Vicki practiced her flying and studied more maps on her walls. She made more calculations, talked to television reporters, and even took international calls!

Soon she was prepared to start her long journey, so Vicki climbed into her plane named **Harmony**, tipped her wings to her friends, and off to Goose Bay, Canada, she flew.

Vicki flew over the blue ocean and rains began to fall. The temperatures did, too, and she had a dangerous close call! The wings took on ice, and the plane almost **stalled**! So she flew under the clouds, and the ice turned to dew. If she hadn't practiced so much and kept calm, she wouldn't have known what to do.

Then she and her instructor flew over giant icebergs and through puffy white clouds to Greenland, where they were greeted by an **Innuit** crowd. The children carried big signs with Vicki's name and welcome greetings high up in the air for her to see. Then they politely lined up single-file to meet her and shake her hand. Even Eskimo dogs licked Vicki's face and her hair!

Then they took off in **Harmony** after their stay and soared over icy waters, through clear skies, now nothing in their way. Over the ice cap they went, almost to the top of the world. They even flew past volcanoes before finally landing in Iceland.

Girl of 12 follows Amelia's flight to glory

94

Record breaker: Vicki salutes her happy landing in Scotland yesterday

Setting goals is what you should

hold a licence, Vicki had to be

French flock to see Vicki on historic flight

By JEAN SHANLEY
TRIBUNE

The old soldiers in Fismes, France had tears in their eyes when Vicki Van Meter arrived.

Vicki, the 12-year-old Meadville girl who piloted a plane across the Atlantic Ocean, was treated like a heroine in Fismes where she delivered a plaque from the city of Meadville to Fismes, its longtime sister city.

James Van Meter, Vicki's father, in a Wednesday evening phone call from Cannes, France, said the presentation and reception in Fismes were "totally awesome." He said the World War I and World War II soldiers who attended the ceremony had tears in their eyes.

A trip was made to a bridge in Fismes where the commemorative plaque will be placed. The bridge is being dedicated to the city of Meadville in September for help the city has given to the residents of Fismes.

Soldiers from Meaville helped liberate Fismes during World War I. During World War II, Meadville residents supported the city with contributions of food and helped those people survive.

Meadville City Council asked Vicki to deliver greetings and the plaque during her European trip.

Next, it was on to Glasgow, Scotland, where lots of press reporters watched Vicki land. Then she continued on to London, England, where more photographers and television cameras were on hand.

Vicki Van Meter, of Meadville, Pennsylvania, at Glasgow Airport last night after becoming the youngest female to fly across the Atlantic

Twelve-year-old flies into the record books

BY ANDREW COLLIER

A GIRL aged 12 stepped on to British soil last night after becoming the youngest female pilot to fly across the Atlantic Ocean.

Vicki Van Meter, who suffers from air-sickness, followed the route of the pioneering aviator Amelia Earhart to make the three-day journey.

At 6.30pm Vicki, from Meadville in Pennsylvania, stepped out of her Cessna 210 aircraft after a perfect landing at Glasgow Airport. Her first reward for making the historic journey was a Biggles flying bear presented by Alexandra Redmond, of the British Women Pilots' Association,

and a framed photograph of the airport presented by Robert Swan, operations director there.

Vicki, who will not qualify for a private pilot's licence until she is 16, made the crossing with her flight instructor, Curt Arnspiger.

The journey, which closely followed Earhart's historic 1932 solo flight across the Atlantic, took her from Newfoundland to Greenland, Iceland and finally Scotland. She was forced to fly close to the sea for part of the journey when the wings of the aircraft began to ice up.

Despite being supervised during the flight, Vicki carried out preparation work, including fuel calculations and

the flight plan, by herself. Her parents, who have spent £7,000 on flying lessons for her, had hoped to witness the landing at Glasgow but were diverted to Ireland because of bad weather.

Vicki's ambition is to become an astronaut. She said last night that she had not been frightened by the Atlantic journey, although it had been "pretty cold".

She added: "I always said it would be hard and it was. It was really exciting.

"I liked the whole flight but soaring over the fjords was....

journey had been undertaken purely for the challenge. Getting her flight officially recorded as a first, she conceded, was likely to be rather difficult, even for a steely and determined 12-year-old "They don't want kids going out and stealing planes, so they don't put underage pilots in *The Guinness Book of Records*".

Vicki, who continues her journey today by flying on to London, Paris, Brussels and Frankfurt....

Triumphant Van Meter embarks on tour of Europe

GLASGOW, Scotland (AP) — Twelve-year-old Vicki Van Meter wasn't resting on her laurels today, as the young pilot prepared to tour Europe fresh from having conquered the Atlantic in her single-engine plane.

The sixth grader from Meadville, Pa., declared it was "pretty neat" to reach Scotland after a three-hop flight from Maine.

"I always thought it would be real hard and it was," she told reporters Tuesday a few minutes after touching down at Glasgow International Airport.

"A lot of people really helped me along the way. They taught me to fly. I didn't do it myself," Vicki said, smiling as she patiently answered questions from a gaggle of journalists and photographers.

But Vicki emphasized that the key to her success has been disciplined goal-setting, "and my trip's not over yet." She planned to set off for Lon-

■ Please turn to 12A/PILOT

AP PHOTO

Meadville's Vicki Van Meter is showered with champagne by flying partner Curt Arnspiger in Glasgow.

In France, the people had a ceremony and a parade. Vicki walked with all the townspeople to the city hall as a marching band played. She wanted to fly as far as she had planned, so she piloted **Harmony** on to Germany, and believe me, she felt mighty good!

When Vicki returned to America, back to her own hometown, tears flowed, pride swelled, the people cheered for her, too. She was in all the papers and went to lots of TV interviews and special events. She even got a letter from the President!

And that's the story of the little girl who wanted to fly. She knew she could do it if only she would try.

The Meadville Tribune
SUNDAY

MEADVILLE, PA.

Van Meter has landed — at home

CHRIS HORNER / Trib...

From a storybook dream to the history books of tomorrow, congratulations!

Listen now,
the girl has a message for you . . .

"Whatever it is you dream to do
BELIEVE
and you can do it, too!
Wherever that journey takes you to
just ask . . .
I'll fly along with you!"

Vicki

Here is a secret that may surprise you . . .
every bit of this story is absolutely true!

Real Story

Victoria 'Vicki' Van Meter took her first flying lesson at the age of 10. In 1993, at the age of 11, accompanied by her instructor Bob Baumgartner, she piloted a single engine Cessna 172 airplane across the United States from Augusta, Maine to San Diego, California, becoming the youngest female to accomplish such a feat. The following year at age 12, accompanied by her instructor Curt Arnspiger, she piloted a single engine Cessna 210 across the Atlantic Ocean from Augusta, Maine to Glasgow, Scotland, continuing on to England, France, and Germany, becoming the only girl to make such a flight. During her flights, she served as an ambassador for her town of Meadville, Pennsylvania, the Commonwealth of Pennsylvania, the city of Augusta, Maine, and also as an honorary ambassador for the United States of America.

After her flights, Vicki spoke with children and adults across the country, inspiring them to follow their dreams. She appeared on numerous television shows, in magazines and newspapers all over the world, and she received the ESPN Arete Award for "superlative courage in sports".

Vicki's picture hangs along with other accomplished women pilots in the Smithsonian National Air and Space Museum in Washington, D.C.

THE WHITE HOUSE

WASHINGTON

September 30, 1993

Vicki Van Meter
902 Grove Street
Meadville, Pennsylvania 16335

Dear Vicki:

    I am delighted to congratulate you on your
record-setting flight.

    I followed your journey closely and cheered
with millions of other Americans as you set three
aviation records: the youngest female pilot to fly
coast-to-coast across the United States, the youngest
pilot to cross the United States from east to west,
and the youngest pilot to set a distance record of
2900 miles.

    As the city of Meadville welcomes you back
and declares this day Vicki Van Meter Day, it
gives me great pleasure to commend you on your
notable achievement. You are an inspiration to
your fellow young Americans, and I know you will
meet future challenges just as you have met this
one -- courageously and successfully.

    Hillary and I send you our best wishes.

Sincerely,

Bill Clinton

THE VICE PRESIDENT

WASHINGTON

May 27, 1994

Ms. Vicki Van Meter
902 Grove Street
Meadville, Pennsylvania 16335

Dear Vicki:

    I was pleased to learn of your plans to fly across the
Atlantic with stops in a number of countries along the way. I
congratulate you on your determination and initiative, and I wish
you well on this very exciting trip.

    As you make the journey, I hope that you will carry a
message of goodwill, best wishes and greetings from your fellow
Americans. The United States is committed to world peace and
mutual cooperation, and we are anxious to work with other nations
so that all of us can enjoy economic prosperity, a clean
environment and an atmosphere of harmony and security.

    Please be assured of my very best wishes and hopes for your
success on this flight and in the years to come.

Sincerely,

Al Gore

AG/wem

Vicki Van Meter's Historic
Trans-Continental Flight
September 20, 1993

Vicki Van Meter's Historic
Trans-Atlantic Flight
June 5, 1994

For more information on Vicki

www.vickivanmeter.com

Glossary

bank the plane: tilting of a plane's wing to change direction

private pilot ground school: a school where pilots learn the rules, regulations, and all the knowledge it takes to be a pilot

Harmony: the name of Vicki's plane on her trans-Atlantic flight

stalled: when a plane loses lift and starts to fall to the ground

Innuits: Eskimo people who inhabit the Arctic

VICTORIA 'VICKI' VAN METER

My Dreams

_____

NAME

and Possibilities